NOBLESVILLE SOUTHEASTERN PUBLIC LIBRARY

P9-BUI-880

j 599.75 Bon 2002
Bonar, Samantha.
Small wildcats

12·03

Small Wildcats

Small Wildcats

Samantha Bonar

Watts LIBRARY™

Franklin Watts
A Division of Scholastic Inc.
New York • Toronto • London • Auckland • Sydney
Mexico City • New Delhi • Hong Kong
Danbury, Connecticut

Hamilton East Public Library
One Library Plaza
Noblesville, IN 46060

For Fluffy, Tiger, and Bear

Note to readers: Definitions for words in **bold** can be found in the Glossary at the back of this book.

Photographs © 2002: BBC Natural History Unit: 14 bottom (G. & H. Denzau), 49 (Jeff Foott), 12 (Owen Newman), 2 (Pete Oxford), 47 (Rico & Ruiz), 28 (Anup Shah), 41 (Rod Williams); Dembinsky Photo Assoc.: 37 (Mary Clay), 9 (Alan G. Nelson), 42 (Jim Roetzel); Minden Pictures: 16 (Jim Brandenburg), 17 (Mitsuaki Iwago), 14 top (Frans Lanting), 43 (Michael Quinton), 25 (Konrad Wothe); Peter Arnold Inc.: cover (Gerard Lacz), 38, 40 (Gunter Ziesler); Photo Researchers, NY: 34 (Francois Gohier), 33 (Tadaaki Imaizumi), 19 (G.C. Kelley), 44 (Wayne Lawler), 11 (Tom McHugh), 5 right, 22 (Jany Sauvanet), 5 left, 6, 26, 29, 31 (Terry Whittaker), 20 (Art Wolfe); Visuals Unlimited/Ken Lucas: 27, 32.

The photograph on the cover shows a bobcat. The photograph opposite the title page shows an ocelot in a tree.

Library of Congress Cataloging-in-Publication Data

Bonar, Samantha.
    Small wildcats / by Samantha Bonar.
        p. cm. — (Watts library)
    Includes bibliographical references and index.
     ISBN 0-531-11965-3 (lib. bdg.)   0-531-16632-5 (lib. bdg.)
    1. Felis—Juvenile literature. [1. Wildcat. 2. Cats.] I. Title. II. Series.
QL737 .C23 B648 2001
599.75'2—dc21

2001017581

©2002 Franklin Watts, a Division of Scholastic Inc.
All rights reserved. Published simultaneously in Canada.
Printed in the United States of America.
1 2 3 4 5 6 7 8 9 10 R 11 10 09 08 07 06 05 04 03 02

Contents

Chapter One
From Fur to Purr 7

Chapter Two
Small Wildcats of Africa 13

Chapter Three
Small Wildcats of Europe and Asia 23

Chapter Four
Small Wildcats of the Americas 35

Chapter Five
Avoiding Catastrophe 45

53 **Glossary**

56 **To Find Out More**

60 **A Note on Sources**

61 **Index**

The rusty-spotted cat is one of the smallest wildcats.

From Fur to Purr

The family of cats is called **Felidae**. This family belongs to the group of mammals called **Carnivora**. These meat-eating mammals also include wolves, bears, raccoons, and seals. Some of the cat's closest relatives are mongooses and hyenas.

No one is sure exactly how many kinds, or **species**, of Felidae there are in the world. They range in size from the tiny 3-pound (1.4-kilogram) rusty-spotted cat of India to the giant 570-pound (258.5-kg) Siberian tiger.

The approximately thirty-six species we know about are divided into three groups called **genuses**. The first group, the **Panthera** genus, consists of the big cats, such as lions, tigers, and jaguars. These big cats are the only ones that are able to roar. The second group, the **Acinonyx** genus, consists of only two species of cheetahs. They are different from the other big cats in that they cannot pull their claws back into sheaths hidden in their paws. The cheetahs' paws are similar to dogs' paws.

Small wildcats make up the third group, or **Felis** genus. There are about twenty-five Felis species, including the common house cat. Although most Felis are small, mountain lions are included in this group because, like all other Felis species, they cannot roar. Genetic studies show that the domestic cat is descended from the African wildcat.

Ferocious Cats

From their thirty sharp teeth to their fierce claws, cats are made for hunting. They all have the same basic skeleton, with small round skulls and long backbones. All Felis species have feet with five toes that have **retractable** claws. Most have lengthy tails. Their shape gives them speed, strength, and an acrobat's grace. Their body proportions vary slightly according to where they live. Jungle cats, like the margay, have shorter limbs that make it easier for them to climb trees, whereas cats, like the serval, that live on open **savannas** have longer legs so they can sprint after prey.

Cats are **predators**, which means they hunt and kill other animals to survive. Their long, muscular legs enable them to run quickly. Even domestic cats can sprint up to 30 miles per hour (48 kilometers per hour). They are able to grasp **prey** with their long front legs and grip it with their sharp claws. With their fierce fangs, they can kill their prey with a bite to the back of the neck.

A lynx catches up to its prey, a snowshoe hare.

What Are Whiskers For?

Cats use the whiskers on their muzzles, cheeks, and above their eyes to help feel their way in the dark. Whiskers contain nerves that are sensitive to movement and touch. A cat's cheek whiskers extend out just a little wider than its body. At this length, the whiskers help the cat judge what spaces it can fit its body through. Whiskers also help cats feel which way their prey goes, if they should lose their grasp of a mouse or bird.

Wildcats hunt mostly at dawn and dusk. With their large eyes, they see much better in dim light than humans do. The colors of wildcats' coats help them blend in with their surroundings so that their prey can't see them as they hide in the bushes. Their ability to fit in with their surroundings also hides them from predators, such as coyotes and wild dogs, that might try to eat them. The Chinese mountain (desert) cat, for example, is the tawny color of sand.

They Want To Be Alone

Wildcats are loners. Most wildcats will not allow another cat of the same sex into their **territory**. Male and female home ranges may overlap, however. Their home base includes a hunting area, sleeping den, water, and lookout points.

Cats generally do not like to fight over territory. So if a cat is challenged by another cat, it usually beats a fast retreat back to its home turf. If a stranger accidentally encounters a resident cat, a brief confrontation may result. One cat will usually surrender by flattening its ears and slinking away.

Generally, cats fight each other only during mating season. When two male cats are fighting over a female cat, both cats may arch their backs to look bigger and more threatening. They may yowl and hiss to try to scare each other off. If these warning tactics don't work, they may have a physical encounter. However, very rarely is a cat seriously injured in one of these brief battles.

Cat Years

Wildcats usually live around ten years, whereas domestic cats can live to be as old as fifteen to twenty years. Here's how to calculate your cat's age in human years.

The first year equals twenty-one human years.

The second year equals ten human years.

Each year thereafter equals three years.

For example, a ten-year-old cat would be fifty-five in human years (21+10+24).

Three Little Kittens—at Least

Wildcats usually mate at the end of winter and give birth between late March and mid-May. They may have another litter in July or early August. The pregnancy lasts about 65 days, during which time the mother cat builds a kind of nest in a den for her young. One to eight kittens are born.

The kittens nurse at first. Then their mother begins hunting for them, bringing prey back to the den. Eventually, the mother teaches the kittens how to kill prey. As they get older, the kittens leave their mother for longer and longer periods. By the time they are six to eight months old, they are ready to leave home and set up their own territories.

Multipurpose Tongue

The cat's tongue is covered with tiny rough hooks that face backward. These serve as little cups when cats drink water and as combs when they groom their fur.

A mother caracal rests with her two kittens.

The serval is one of the many wildcats found on the continent of Africa.

Chapter Two

Small Wildcats of Africa

Small wildcats live in all parts of Africa, from the sand dunes of the Sahara Desert to the grasslands of Tanzania to the rain forests in the center of the continent. Many of these wildcats are master hunters and can jump high, wade through water, or dig in the ground to catch their prey. Some of the wildcats rely on their prey for both their food and water.

One black-footed cat rests in a hollow termite hill while another cat approaches.

This photograph (below) shows how well a sand cat blends in with its environment.

Desert Dwellers

The black-footed cat often sleeps in hollow termite hills. It is sometimes called the anthill tiger. The soft pads on the undersides of its feet, which allow cats to sneak up on their prey, are black. Weighing from 2 to 5 pounds (0.9 to 2.3 kg), it is the smallest of the African wildcats.

Found only in the southern tip of Africa, the black-footed cat prefers desert habitats with little vegetation. It does not need to drink water, getting all it needs from its prey, which include rodents, lizards, and beetles. This fierce predator sometimes attacks mammals much larger than itself. The black-footed cat is rare.

Like the black-footed cat, the sand cat gets all the water it needs from its prey, mostly gerbils. It has thick fur on the underside of its paws to protect it from hot sand. The sand cat is known for its large, fox-like ears. Its sand-colored coat helps it blend into the deserts of North Africa and the Arabian Peninsula, from Algeria to Palestine. It

Cat Chat

For the most part, wildcats are silent creatures. As kittens, they meow only to get their mother's attention. As adults, the only time they make a racket is during mating season, when male cats let out loud **caterwauls**. When threatened, wildcats snarl or hiss, and occasionally adults, like kittens, purr when they are happy.

Cats also use their body language to communicate. For example, cats flick the end of their tails to show that they are annoyed. Flattened ears means they are feeling threatened.

burrows into the sand to sleep during the day and hunts when temperatures cool at night. Weighing up to 7.5 pounds (3.4 kg), it is about the size of a domestic cat.

Unlike most cats, which do not use **vocalizations** to communicate, sand cats contact each other with a short bark-like sound. They are more social than other cat species. Males have overlapping territories and take turns using dens. Because of their docile personalities, they have been trapped as pets, but they do not live long in captivity. Their numbers in the wild are dwindling.

Cat of the Grasslands

The caracal was named for its unique ears. *Caracal* is from the Turkish word meaning "black ear," and caracals are known for their long, pointed ears tipped with black tufts. The tufts may help the caracal pinpoint sounds, or the caracal may move the tufts to communicate with other caracals. An ear flick seems to be used as a mild threat.

It is easy to tell a caracal by its distinctive ears.

The caracal is also famous for its acrobatics. It is so good at leaping several feet straight up after birds that Indian moguls used to place bets on how many pigeons a tame caracal could knock down out of the air.

Caracals are found all over Africa, particularly in dry woodland and **savanna**, in countries such as Sudan, Namibia, Gabon, Ethiopia, and Nigeria. They also live in the Middle East and southwestern Asia. Most have reddish fur, but sometimes they are black.

The largest of the African small cats, the caracal is about the size of a Labrador dog. It weighs up to 40 pounds (18 kg). It is big enough to kill small antelopes, but more often it eats rodents, hares, and birds. Because they sometimes eat sheep, caracals are persecuted by farmers. Despite this, they are not **endangered**.

Bouncing Along

The serval has the largest, most rounded ears of the wildcats. It uses its big ears to listen for prey while hiding in the grass. Because of its long neck and legs, the serval has been called the giraffe cat. It lives in sub-Saharan Africa in wet environments with tall grass, such as reed beds along rivers. Among other countries, it is found in Mozambique, Ethiopia, Tanzania, Botswana, and Togo.

Servals are known for bounding through the grass with high bouncing steps to flush animals from cover. These master hunters also dig for prey underground and wade in shallow

Follow Your Ears

When hunting, cats rely more on their hearing than their sense of smell. More than twenty ear muscles help them turn their ears like satellite dishes to the source of a sound. This helps them figure out quickly where the sound is coming from.

A serval leaps to attack its prey in the grass.

water to catch birds, such as flamingos, as well as frogs and fish.

One of the larger of the small wildcats, servals weigh from 20 to 40 pounds (9 to 18 kg). Males are very territorial. In a confrontation, two males sit and face each other. One serval taps the other's chest with his paw. The other serval may bite the paw. Sometimes a fight ensues, but more often the two engage in a staring contest until one backs down.

Although it is hunted for its beautiful tawny-gold, black-spotted coat, the serval's population is widespread throughout Africa. It is not considered threatened.

Forest Cats

The wildcat, a stocky tabby-like cat, is the ancestor of all domestic cats. It is easily tamed and the pet of many African farmers. Weighing 8 to 12 pounds (3.6 to 5.4 kg), the wildcat is found in forests, grasslands, and deserts throughout Africa and the Middle East, as well as in parts of Asia and Europe. It hunts at night and eats rodents, reptiles, amphibians, birds, and insects. Scientists estimate there are about 100,000 wild-cats left.

Cat Beginnings

Cats first appeared on Earth about 40 million years ago. About 6,000 years ago, wildcats in Africa began wandering into human settlements in search of food. Some of these wildcats began living with humans, becoming **domesticated**, or tame.

All of the domestic cats that people keep as pets descended from the wildcat.

The African golden cat lives in the rain forests of Africa.

Sacred Cats

The ancient Egyptians not only loved cats—they worshipped them. By 1600 B.C., cats were considered sacred animals, and they are depicted in Egyptian art dating to this period. The Egyptians even had a goddess, Bast, who had the head of a cat and the body of a woman. Cats were bred and lived in sacred temples, but they were also cherished family pets. When a pet cat died, family members shaved off their eyebrows as a sign of grief. They then gave their cats funerals and mummified their remains the same way they did humans', wrapping them in linen. More than 30,000 cat mummies were found in one ancient Egyptian town by archeologists. The punishment for killing a cat was death.

The African golden cat is another small wildcat that can be found in African forests. It lives in the rain forests and eats monkeys, as well as birds, rodents, and small deer. About twice as big as a domestic cat, African golden cats are found in central and western Africa, including the Congo Republic and Uganda. They sleep in trees during the day and hunt at dawn and dusk. They are very secretive and have never been studied in the wild. Little is known about their numbers, but they are thought to be in danger because of the extensive habitat destruction occurring throughout Africa.

The European wildcat is known for its thick, ringed tail.

Chapter Three

Small Wildcats of Europe and Asia

From the misty forests of Scotland to the steamy jungles of Southeast Asia, many varieties of wildcats, such as the Eurasian lynx and the Iriomote cat, live their solitary lives on the vast Eurasian continent and its islands.

European Cats

Slightly larger than a domestic cat, the European wildcat is a tabby with a black-ringed bushy tail tipped with black. It is found from Germany southward to the Mediterranean islands as well as in Scotland and southwestern Asia. It weighs from 8 to 12 pounds (3.6 to 5.4 kg). Its numbers have declined dramatically in recent years because of agriculture and **deforestation**. European wildcats most commonly live in forests but can survive in a wide variety of habitats, including swampy areas.

The wildcat's main diet consists of rodents, rabbits, and other small mammals, which it mostly hunts at night. It also eats birds. The wildcat's hunting of birds once caused its persecution by gamekeepers because it would steal the chicks of **game birds** and chicken. It is not targeted so much any more, however, because people have realized that the wildcats control forest rodents that damage trees.

Wildcats Almost Everywhere!

Wildcats are native to every continent except Australia and Antarctica, and the islands of the West Indies and Madagascar.

Home on the Range

The largest of the European wildcats and the largest of all lynx species, the Eurasian lynx weighs from 40 to 48 pounds (18 to 22 kg). This bob-tailed feline is found in the forests, scrub woodland, and rocky hills of northern Europe, Russia, and central Asia. Tawny with black spots and black tufts on its ear tips, this cat prefers large prey, such as deer. It also hunts hares and chamois (a kind of mountain goat).

The home range of the lynx can be as large as 115 square miles (297.8 square kilometers). Wildcats mark their territory

by using their scent to let other cats know they have crossed their boundaries. They do so by spraying urine and depositing feces. They also have special glands that release their scent in their chins, cheeks, and tails, which they rub against objects within their territory. Leaving scratch marks on trees, which is called claw-raking, is a visual way for a lynx to warn other cats that this is its area. Scratching trees also releases scent from glands in the paws. The Eurasian lynx, like other wildcats, checks on its territory several times every day to examine the scent spots for intruders. Although it is **vulnerable** in some areas, the Eurasian lynx population is largely stable.

The Eurasian lynx is one of the largest wildcats in Europe.

A rusty-spotted cat carries its next meal in its jaws—a mouse.

Asian Cats

One of the tiniest of all the wildcats, the rusty-spotted cat could easily fit in a shoebox. Found in India and Sri Lanka, this cat is less than half the size of a domestic cat, weighing only 3 pounds (1.4 kg) and measuring 7 inches (17.8 centimeters) high at the shoulders. Its grayish fur is spotted with reddish blotches.

The rusty-spotted cat lives in dry, open forests and grasslands. Sometimes it is found in villages, where it has been known to steal chickens and occasionally has been discovered living in abandoned houses. The rusty-spotted cat hunts at night and likes to eat small mammals, birds, reptiles, frogs, and even insects. This wildcat is a good tree climber and is said to be very playful. Sometimes, it is tamed and kept as a pet.

Little is known about another Asian cat, the rare Chinese mountain (desert) cat. It lives in the alpine meadows and scrublands of the northeastern edge of the Tibetan plateau in China. Larger than a domestic cat, the Chinese mountain cat has a thick grayish-yellow coat that is white to whitish-gray on the underside. During the day, it sleeps in burrows, coming out only at night to hunt rodents. It is in danger of becoming **extinct** because of hunting and rodent-poisoning programs.

Found in the rocky alpine deserts and high-altitude grasslands of central Asia, the Pallas's cat must survive in cold, dry terrain. The fur on its tail and underside is twice the length of the fur on its back to protect it from the cold ground. The

The homeland of the Pallas's cat's starts around the Caspian Sea and stretches to central China and Mongolia.

4- to 10-pound (1.8- to 4.5-kg) Pallas's cat preys on mammals and birds. It is able to climb rocks with ease. It has large, round eyes like an owl, and its coat is light gray to yellowish buff, with white tips that make it look frosted with a light dusting of snow.

Unlike other wildcats, Pallas's cat is a social animal. The cats greet each other by body rubbing. Their population is vulnerable because of illegal hunting for their fur and rodent-poisoning programs.

The paws of a jungle cat are its main instrument for hunting.

Swimming Cats

Unlike most cats, jungle cats love water. These cats will dive right in to catch fish or escape from dogs. They live in marshes near streams and rivers from the Middle East to India and Southeast Asia. Weighing from 8 to 13 pounds (3.6 to 5.9 kg), these strong swimmers have large, cone-shaped ears and tawny coats with white bellies. Although they are on the small side, jungle cats hunt young deer and pigs in addition to large rodents, and they have been known to eat porcupines and snakes.

Ancient Egyptians trained jungle cats to hunt wildfowl. Jungle cat mummies have been found in tombs. The males of the species make loud howls that sound like barks. Their population is stable.

Another strong swimmer is the flat-headed cat, which lives in swampy areas in Thailand, Malaysia, Sumatra, and Borneo. With its partially webbed paws acting like scoops, it is a great fisher. The flat-headed cat enjoys sitting in water and washing objects. It eats fish, frogs, and the occasional bird. It also shows a fondness for fruit and digs up sweet potatoes to eat. Its head is broad and flat with unusually small ears. The cat's thick fur is reddish. Weighing 3 to 5.5 pounds (1.4 to 2.5 kg), this little swimmer faces an uncertain future because of water pollution.

The fishing cat will dive into water and swim after fish, grabbing them with its mouth. This mostly nocturnal cat sometimes uses a tree branch as a diving board. It also taps the

A fishing cat swims in the water in search of food while behind it another fishing cat eats its prey on shore.

surface of the water with its paws to attract fish, then scoops them out. It lives in swamps and eats frogs and snakes as well as fish, crabs, and even shellfish.

About the size of a basset hound, the 13- to 26-pound (5.9- to 11.8-kg) cat is found from northern India to Southeast Asia. With a gray coat spotted and striped with black, it looks like a domestic tabby cat. Although the species is not threatened, fishers and farmers often trap and kill these cats.

The Most Beautiful Fur

Temminck's golden cat is one of the larger wildcats, weighing 19 to 33 pounds (8.6 to 14.9 kg). It has a beautiful golden brown coat, which sometimes is a bright golden red. Black cats are a common variation. Found in Southeast Asia from Nepal, Tibet, Thailand, and Malaysia to Sumatra, the golden cat lives in tropical rain forests, deciduous forests, and other habitats. This dog-sized cat hunts large rodents, hares, birds, and lizards. It can also kill larger prey, such as small deer, sheep, goats, and newborn water buffalo calves.

Bornean Bay Cat

The most mysterious of the wildcats is the Bornean bay cat, only one of which has been seen and collected, in 1992. A few skulls and skins have been found. This small red cat—6 to 9 pounds (2.7 to 4.1 kg)—is believed to live in dense tropical forests on the island of Borneo and is thought to be endangered because its habitats are being destroyed. Some scientists think it may be a smaller version of the Asiatic golden cat.

These cats are threatened because of **habitat** destruction and because they are illegally hunted for their fur. Some people in Thailand, who call the golden cat the fire tiger, believe that carrying a golden cat hair will keep tigers away. Others believe that eating the cat will accomplish the same goal.

Another small wildcat that is hunted for its beautiful coat is the leopard cat. It is one of the most commonly found wildcats, living all over Southeast Asia from scrublands to woods to semi-deserts. It is found as far north as North Korea and as far south as Bali, as well as in India, Bangladesh, Burma, Indochina, the Philippines, Borneo, Java, and islands near Japan. The 6- to 8-pound (2.7- to 3.6-kg) cat eats small mammals, reptiles, insects, amphibians, birds, fish, deer fawns, eggs, and grass. The leopard cat is itself the prey of leopards.

Leopard cats sometimes live near villages and go on poultry-stealing

The survival of the Temminck's golden cat is threatened by hunters who kill the animal for its fur.

A leopard cat curls up on a rock to take a rest.

raids. The Chinese call it the money cat because its round spots remind them of coins. These cats are excellent tree-climbers and swimmers. They do not appear to be endangered.

The small marbled cat prefers moist tropical forests where it can climb trees. It is fairly small in size, weighs only 5 to 15 pounds (2.3 to 6.8 kg), and has brownish yellow fur with black blotches. Its long tail helps it balance in trees, where it does most of its hunting. Found from northern India to Nepal and Indonesia, the marbled cat eats birds, frogs, lizards, and rodents. It is very rare and extremely vulnerable to extinction because of the rapid destruction of tropical forests in Southeast Asia.

On the Verge of Extinction

With only about one hundred left, the Iriomote cat is on the verge of extinction. About the size of the domestic cat, the Iriomote cat has tabby markings. This cat is found only on the Japanese island of Iriomotejima, in rain forests and near water. About one-third of its diet consists of insects, including thirty-nine different kinds of beetles. It also eats bats, rats, wild pigs, herons, owls, fish, and turtles—more than ninety-five different kinds of animals in all. It enjoys swimming and playing in water.

Although one-third of the island has been declared a reserve and the cat was declared a national Japanese treasure, its numbers continue to decline due to hunting and habitat destruction. Unfortunately, islanders consider its meat a delicacy.

An ocelot stops at a water hole for a drink.

Chapter Four

Small Wildcats of the Americas

There are many tiny tigers and little leopards in South American jungles and forests. Many of these spotted and striped cats have cousins that are all black. Spotted coats, like the ocelot's, mimic the splotches of light and shadow found in a forest. All-black cats often live in very dense forests where little sunlight filters through. The only uniquely North

American small wildcats are the bobcat and the Canadian lynx.

Rain Forest Dwellers

The ocelot looks like a miniature leopard and can be found throughout Central and South America, including Colombia, Ecuador, Peru, and Argentina. It used to be common in the southern United States, but now it is found only in southern Texas and Arizona. In the last century, it was trapped so extensively for its beautiful spotted fur that its North American population was almost wiped out. While trade in ocelot pelts now is prohibited, its numbers have continued to decrease because of habitat loss.

About twice the size of a domestic cat at 15 to 30 pounds (6.8 to 13.6 kg), the ocelot was once a popular pet in North America. There is some speculation that southern Florida may have a population of wild ocelots made up of escaped pets.

A solitary, nocturnal hunter, the ocelot stalks rabbits and rodents on the ground and birds in trees. It also eats insects, land crabs, and fish, and it needs to hunt up to 12 hours a day to get enough food. It even has been known to eat squirrel monkeys, armadillos, and crocodiles. In the daytime, it sleeps in trees.

The oncilla, or tiger cat, lives high on South American mountains in misty cloud forests. The rare black-spotted cat lives on the ground but is a very good tree climber. This tiny wildcat—4 to 6.5 pounds (1.8 to 2.9 kg)—feeds on birds,

reptiles, insects, and rodents. It has a very long tail, almost as long as its entire torso. It is found in Costa Rica, Venezuela, Brazil, Colombia, Bolivia, and Argentina. Oncillas were once hunted for their pelts, but trade in oncilla products has been outlawed. This wildcat faces a new threat, however: a coffee plantations are replacing the high-altitude forests where it lives.

An ocelot spends half of each day searching for food.

Acrobatic Cats

The margay, a tiny tree-dwelling cat, has such flexible ankles it can climb down trees headfirst like a squirrel. It also can hang from a branch by one foot while hunting tree rats, squirrels, opossums, tree frogs, and birds. Weighing about 7 pounds (3.2 kg), it is found in forests from southern Mexico to

Showing off its climbing skills, a margay works its way up a tree.

northern Argentina. It once was found in Texas but is now extinct there. Its tail, which is even longer than the oncilla's, helps it balance in trees. Once popular as pets and hunted for their pelts, margays are now considered in danger of becoming extinct and are protected.

A fantastic tree-climber, Geoffroy's cat has been seen walking upside-down along a branch and hanging by its back feet. It also sleeps and hunts in trees and is a good swimmer. Found in dense, scrubby areas along rivers in the southern half of

South America, it is active during the day as well as the night. It hunts rodents, hares, lizards, insects, and birds.

Weighing 9 to 11 pounds (4.1 to 4.9 kg), Geoffroy's cat looks similar to a domestic cat. It has a handsome yellow or silver coat with black spots (or all-black). Thousands of Geoffroy's cats have been killed for their fur. In the three-year period between 1976 and 1979, 350,000 skins were exported from Argentina alone. Although hunting is now prohibited, the numbers of this wildcat continue to decline.

Fluffy Fur Keeps Them Warm

The pampas cat is one of the only small wildcats with long fur. It sometimes even has a little mane. Striped like a tabby and weighing 6 to 9 pounds (2.7 to 4.1 kg), it looks similar to the African wildcat and the domestic cat. Some all-black individuals have been seen.

The pampas cat is found in open grassy areas, scrublands, forests, and mountain regions in Brazil, Chile, Peru, Bolivia, Ecuador, and Argentina. It eats mainly small mammals, such as guinea pigs, although it has been seen stealing penguin eggs in Patagonia. Its **conservation** status is uncertain, but it may be endangered because of illegal hunting and the destruction of its habitats to make way for farming.

At 4 pounds (1.8 kg), the kodkod is the smallest cat of the Americas, about half the size of a domestic cat. It is closely related to Geoffroy's cat and the pampas cat and looks like a smaller version of those species. It is found in Argentina and

The Andean mountain cat's long fur helps protect it in the cold climate of its habitat.

Chile. Kodkods live in pine forests and hunt small **nocturnal** mammals and birds. They are social cats and may even live together. The kodkod is very rare in the wild and is facing extinction due to habitat destruction.

The Andean mountain cat, which usually weighs 8 to 9 pounds (3.6 to 4.1 kg), lives high in the cold Andes Mountains of South America. It has long, soft, gray fur to keep it warm in the rocky, treeless, windy areas where it lives. Its tail is bushy and ringed like a raccoon's. Because it lives in such hard-to-reach places, it is difficult to study and little is known about this small wildcat. It eats small mammals, lizards, and birds. Its numbers are uncertain, and so it has protected status.

Is This a Cat?

The jaguarundi may be very strange looking, but it is a cat. With its long body and short legs, it resembles a weasel. In Mexico, it is called the otter cat. At 9 to 15 pounds (4.1 to 6.8 kg), it is slightly larger than a domestic cat. Its coat color is solid, either reddish or dark gray.

Jaguarundis are found all over South America, as well as in Arizona and Texas and parts of Central America. There also has been a wild population in Florida since the 1940s. They live in forests, swampy areas, and shrubland and are often found near rivers. Although they mostly hunt on the ground, they are superb climbers and swimmers. They are primarily active at twilight, and their solid-colored coats help them blend into the shadows. Rabbits, rodents, reptiles, birds, armadillos, fruit, and insects form their diet.

The jaguarundi's conservation status is unknown, though it is thought to be common.

The thick fur on the paws of the Canadian lynx helps protect its feet in the snow.

Coming to America

Domesticated cats came to America on ships when families immigrated from Europe starting in the 1700s. In 1749, a special shipment of cats was sent to Pennsylvania to help combat a serious rat problem.

Wildcats of North America

The Canadian lynx is specially adapted for life in the snow. Its large feet are covered with long fur and act as snowshoes, allowing it to move across deep snow easily. Its coat is reddish brown, and the hairs are tipped with white. It is found in forests across Canada into Alaska, and in the Rocky Mountains of the United States.

The Canadian lynx eats mostly snowshoe hares. Adults can weigh from 20 to 24 pounds (9.1 to 10.8 kg). The species is not endangered.

Found from southern Canada to Central Mexico, the bobcat is a relative of the Canadian lynx. It lives all over the United States, in forests, mountains, semi-deserts, and subtropical swamps, but is most common in the western states. It has a short tail and a tan coat with dark spots.

The bobcat is not a picky eater, dining on grasshoppers, beetles, prairie dogs, porcupines, bats, snakes, and birds. It also has been known to eat domestic cats, dogs, sheep, goats, poultry, grass, cactus apples, grapes, and pears. Its diet is roughly 60 to 65 percent rabbits, 20 to 25 percent rodents, and 2 percent reptiles and insects. It likes catnip as much as domestic cats do. The larger male bobcats can weigh up to 29 pounds (13.2 kg) and are able to kill deer. Females can weigh as little as 13 pounds (5.9 kg).

Bobcats live in dens in rocks, hollow trees, or bushes, swim in streams, and rest in trees. Although frequently trapped for their fur, their population is stable.

A young bobcat plays with its food, a horned lark.

Many of the world's small wildcats are facing extinction because of the destruction of their habitats.

Chapter Five

Avoiding Catastrophe

According to the World Conservation Union, wildcat populations "have long been in decline," and today their numbers continue to dwindle rapidly. Much of the decline can be attributed largely to the loss of wildcat habitats. Cats are very sensitive to changes in their environment. When the forests and grasslands where wildcats live are destroyed to make room for houses or farms, there is less food for them and there is not enough shelter to protect them from the elements and predators. The amount of the land available for wildcat habitats around the world is decreasing every day.

In addition to the loss of habitat, wildcats face another threat—humans. People most often hunt wildcats for their fur, but also because the cats sometimes kill farmers' livestock. People also hunt wildcats for sport or for food.

The good news is that many people and organizations are trying to help wildcats survive. Organizations want to study cats in the wild because only in this way can people figure out what the wildcats need to survive. People around the world are working to preserve the cats' natural habitat and to stop illegal killing of wildcats. Efforts are also being made to preserve wildcats in zoos and shelters.

The **Cat Specialist Group**, which is a part of the World Conservation Union, is sponsoring projects all over the world to study and save wildcats, from the African golden cat to the flat-headed cat. The Cat Specialist Group is a panel of nearly two hundred scientists, wildlife managers, and other specialists from forty countries who have volunteered their expertise to the Species Survival Commission. The group provides other organizations with information and advice concerning wildcats. Cat Specialist Group members currently are involved in the study of nearly thirty different small cat species.

Cats in Trouble

The Convention on International Trade in Endangered Species of Flora and Fauna (CITES), an international treaty established in 1973 to control and monitor trading in animals and plants, determines which species are endangered. Those included in Appendix I are the most endangered. These animals are threatened with extinction. Animals in Appendix II are at serious risk and need protection. Trade in animals listed in Appendixes I and II is not allowed. CITES member countries meet once every two years to discuss the animals and update the appendixes as needed.

According to CITES, the most threatened small wildcat is the Spanish lynx. Only about 1,200 are left in Spain and 100 in Portugal. Their numbers are expected to decline by 20 percent in the next decade due to habitat loss and to reduced numbers of the European rabbit, which is their main food

This photograph shows a Spanish lynx, which is considered the most endangered small wildcat.

source. Another danger to the lynx comes from the traps people set to catch rabbits. These same traps also kill a large number of lynx. The Spanish government is developing a conservation plan that would ban rabbit traps. A captive breeding program is already underway. The fine for killing a Spanish lynx is $8,000.

The second most threatened wildcat is Japan's Iriomote cat. Less than one hundred may be left, largely because of habitat loss. The Japanese government is planning action to save this rare cat.

No Place to Sleep, Nothing to Eat

Temminck's golden cat and the Bornean bay cat are examples of cats that are endangered because their habitats are being destroyed. Both are very rare, and their numbers are further threatened by loss of their forest homes.

Sri Lanka's tiny rusty-spotted cat is extremely rare. It may be dying out due to deforestation. Asia's fishing cat is at risk because of the destruction of wetlands and pollution, which poisons its prey. More than half of the fishing cat's habitat is threatened. Destruction of rain forests threatens South America's marbled cat, margay, and oncilla.

The African golden cat is threatened because its prey, a small antelope, is so widely hunted by people for food that there is not enough left for the cats. Asia's flat-headed cat is rare and getting rarer because of water pollution, which poisons its prey. Large-scale poisoning of pikas, a rodent that is

Facing Extinction

IUCN Cat Specialist Group has identified the following small wildcats are the most vulnerable:
Spanish lynx
Iriomote cat
Bornean bay cat
Chinese mountain cat
Black-footed cat
Kodkod
Andean mountain cat
Flat-headed cat
Fishing cat
African golden cat
Asiatic golden cat
Oncilla
Rusty-spotted cat
Marbled cat

the Chinese mountain cat's main source of food, is killing these cats as well. The rare black-footed cat of Africa is threatened by poisoning of locusts and other food sources.

Pallas's cat has long been hunted for its long fur coat. In the early 1900s in Mongolia, as many as 50,000 were killed every year. Although there has been little recent trade in Pallas's cat fur, the cat has almost disappeared in certain areas due to hunting.

Many South American cats, such as the margay, oncilla, and Geoffroy's cat, are still hunted illegally for their spotted fur. Around the world, hundreds of thousands of small cats are killed every year for their fur.

A stand in a market in Ecuador offers ocelot and other animal skins for sale.

Safe—For Now

Some of the least threatened wildcats are Asia's sand cat, which lives in the desert and is not sought after by humans. The caracal is common throughout Africa. The adaptable Canadian lynx and bobcat are in good shape, as are South America's jaguarundi and leopard cat. Ocelots, which once were killed at a rate of as many as 200,000 a year for their fur, have bounced back since hunting these wildcats was banned. There could be as many as 3 million ocelots in the South American forests, though about 7,000 a year are still killed illegally.

Servals benefit from the increased rodent population that comes along with human settlements. An adult serval can eat about 4,000 rodents a year.

Interbreeding Cats

Even though the African and European wildcat is the most common variety of small wildcat, increased breeding with domestic cats is making pure wildcats rare. The Wildlife Conservation Research Unit (WildCRU) of the Department of Zoology at the University of Oxford in England is tracking the behavior and studying the biology of wildcats in Scotland.

If Scottish wildcats and domestic cats are found to be practically identical, so there won't be a need to try to preserve the wildcat as a distinct species. However, if they are found to be genetically different, measures controlling domestic and feral cats could be put in place, such as neutering all domestic cats in certain areas. The African wildcat faces this same problem of interbreeding, or **hybridization**.

How You Can Help Wildcats

The Cat Survival Trust, a charity organization started in Hertfordshire, England, in 1976, promotes the conservation of wildcats. It focuses on preserving the wildcats' habitat and raises money to buy habitat in countries around the world. The first reserve the trust bought was in Misiones, Argentina, where five species of wildcats—jaguarundi, ocelot, margay, puma, and tiger cat—live in the forest. The trust is at present seeking to buy 300,000 acres (121,406 hectares) in seven different countries to set aside as reserves.

To help fund these projects, you can sponsor one of the forty wildcats at the trust's shelter in Hertfordshire. The trust will send you a certificate and updates about your cat.

The Feline Conservation Center in Rosamond, California, houses about sixty endangered wildcats from around the world. Cubs born at this nonprofit center are often sent to zoos or breeding programs. The center also works with the Cat Specialist Group to help conserve cats in the wild. You can adopt a cat by paying for its care each month. You will receive a picture of your cat, and your name will be mounted on a plaque on their cage. Among the residents of the Feline Conservation Center are a fishing cat named Frisbee and an ocelot named Fuzz.

Pallas's Cat Project

Wild About Cats is sponsoring a study of Pallas's cat in Mongolia, headed by Ohio State University veterinary student Meredith Brown. Eighty percent of Pallas's kittens born in captivity in the last three years have died from a parasite called *Toxoplasma gondii*, and Brown wants to find out why in order to better protect Pallas's cats in zoos. Brown and her team trap the cats and take blood, fecal, and skin samples to gain information about their health. Then they examine the samples for parasites and other health factors.

51

Noblesville Southeastern Public Library

Wild About Cats in Auburn, California, shelters wildcats and sponsors research and conservation programs. At present it is sponsoring the creation of the first margay refuge in northern Ecuador and funding scientists studying Pallas's cat in Mongolia.

The International Society for Endangered Cats (ISEC) in Canada, associated with the Cat Specialist Group, is a captive breeding program that houses the world's largest collection of small wildcats. It also helps set up breeding programs in other countries. You may sponsor one of their sand cats, margays, oncillas, or others.

Glossary

Acinonyx—the genus containing the two cheetah species

Carnivora—The scientific order, or group, of animals that eat meat, including cats, wolves, and bears

caterwaul—a loud cry

Cat Specialist Group—a branch of the World Conservation Union specializing in studying and preserving wildcats

conservation—the protection and preservation of endangered animals and their habitats

deforestation—the process of clearing forest land or having cleared forest land

domesticated—tamed wild animals that live in close association with humans

endangered—animals who are in danger of extinction and

whose survival is unlikely if current circumstances do not change

extinct—a species that has not been seen in the wild in the last fifty years

family—a group of similar animals containing several genera. See genus.

Felidae—the scientific name for the family of all cats, large and small

Felis—the genus containing the small cats, including the house cat

game bird—any type of bird that is hunted, excluding waterfowl such as ducks and geese

genus—a subdivision of a family of animals containing more than one species

habitat—the kind of area where an animal lives, such as desert or grassland

hybridization—the interbreeding between different species, such as wild and domestic cats

nocturnal—active at night

Panthera—the genus made up of most of the large cats

predator—an animal that hunts other animals for food

prey—an animal that is hunted or caught for food

retractable—able to draw back or in

savanna—a flat, grassy plain with few trees

species—a distinct kind of animal. The ocelot is one species, for example. Members of a species look alike and breed with each other.

territory—the cat's home range, including hunting grounds, sleeping den, water, and lookout points

vocalization—making a sound

vulnerable—a species that is likely to move into the endangered category in the near future

To Find Out More

Books

Arnold, Carol. *Cats: In from the Wild*. Minneapolis, MN: Carolrhoda Books Inc, 1993.

Kitchener, Andrew. *The Natural History of the Wild Cats*. Ithaca, New York: Cornell University Press, 1991.

Lumpkin, Susan. *Small Cats*. New York: Facts on File, 1993.

Ryden, H. *Your Cat's Wild Cousins*. New York: Lodestar Books, Dutton, 1991.

Wild Discovery Guide to Your Cat: Understanding and Caring for the Tiger Within. New York: Discovery Books, 1999.

Organizations and Online Sites

Cat Specialist Group
Species Survival Commission of IUCN
World Conservation Commission
Avenue du Mont-Blanc
1196 Gland, Switzerland
The Cat Specialist Group of the World Conservation Commission is sponsoring projects all over the world to study and save wildcats.

The Cat Survival Trust
The Centre, Codicote Road
Welwyn, AL6 9TU, England
http://members.aol.com/_ht_a/cattrust/
This charity focuses on preserving the habitat where wildcats live.

CITES Secretariat
International Environment House, 15
Chemin des Anemones, CH-1219
Chatelaine-Geneva, Switzerland
http://www.cites.org
The Convention on International Trade in Endangered Species of Flora and Fauna (CITES) is an international treaty established in 1973 to control and monitor trading in animals

and plants. It figures out which species are endangered. Member countries meet every two years for updates.

Defenders of Wildlife
1101 Fourteenth Street NW, Suite 1400
Washington, DC 20005
http://www.defenders.org
This non-profit organization is dedicated to protecting wild animals and plants in their native environments.

Feline Conservation Center
HCR 1, Box 84
Rosamond, CA 93560-9705
http://www.cathouse-fcc.org
The center houses endangered wildcats and provides cubs to zoos and breeding programs. It also helps conserve cats in the wild.

ISEC Canada
P.O. Box 49004
Ogden RPO
Calgary, Alberta, Canada
http://www.wildcatconservation.org
The International Society for Endangered Cats (ISEC) in Canada is a captive breeding program that houses the world's largest collection of small wildcats. It also helps set up breeding programs in other countries.

National Wildlife Federation
1400 Sixteenth Street NW
Washington, DC 20037
http://www.nwf.org
This conservation organization works to protect wildlife and
the environment.

Natural History Museum of Los Angeles County
http://www.lam.mus.ca.us/cats/
The museum Web site features information from its "Cats:
From Wild to Mild" exhibit.

Wild About Cats
P.O. Box 9182
Auburn, CA 95604
http://www.wildaboutcats.org
This organization shelters wildcats and sponsors research and
conservation programs.

World Wildlife Fund
1250 24th Street NW
Washington, DC 20037
http://www.worldwildlife.org
This international conservation organization works to protect
endangered species and places and to address global threats to
these species and places.

A Note on Sources

Andrew Kitchener's *The Natural History of the Wild Cats* explores the subject of wildcats in great depth, particularly what he calls the neglected small ones. At 280 pages, it is filled with useful and interesting information for the more advanced reader. Kitchener is curator of mammals and birds at the Royal Museum of Scotland in Edinburgh. Animal behaviorist Susan Lumpkin's *Small Cats* is also a comprehensive resource that includes many excellent photographs. Her book is suitable for all ages.

For more up-to-date information, try the Natural History Museum of Los Angeles County's small cats Web site, which is based on their recent exhibit, "Cats: From Wild to Mild." It has very good general information and includes classroom exercises. For older readers, the Cat Survival Trust's Web site has more in-depth information about specific small wildcats, including the latest conservation data.

—*Samantha Bonar*

Index

Numbers in *italics* indicate illustrations.

Acinonyx genus, 8
African golden cats *20*, 21
    prey, 48
African wildcats, 18, *19*
Andean mountain cats, 40, *40*

black-footed cats, *14*
    feet, 14
    prey, 14, 49
bobcats, 36, *43*, 50
    fur, 43
    habitat, 43
    prey, 43, *43*
    size, 43
body language, 15
Bornean bay cats, 30
    habitat, 30, 48
    size, 30

Canadian lynx, 36, *42*, 50
    fur, 42

habitat, 42
prey, 42
size, 42
caracals, *11*, 15–17, *16*, 50
    habitat, 16
    prey, 16–17
    size, 16
Carnivora mammals, 7
Cat Specialist Group, 46,
    51
Cat Survival Trust, 51
caterwauls, 15
Chinese mountain cats, 27
    fur, 10, 27
    prey, 27, 49
claw-raking, 25
claws, 8
Convention on International
    Trade in Endangered
    Species of Flora and
    Fauna (CITES), 46–47

dens, 11, 15

ears, 15, *16*, 17
endangered species, 47, 48
Eurasian lynx, *25*
  habitat, 24
  prey, 24
  size, 24
  territories, 24–25
European wildcats, *22*
  habitat, 24
  prey, 24
  size, 24
eyes, 10

feet, 8, 14
Felidae family, 7
Feline Conservation Center, 51
Felis genus, 8
females, 10, 11
fire tigers. *See* Temminck's golden cats.
fishing cats, 28–29, *29*
  fur, 30
  habitat, 30, 48
  prey, 29, *29*, 30
  size, 30
flat-headed cats, 29
  habitat, 48

Geoffroy's cats, 38–39
  fur, 39, 49
grooming, 11

hunting, 9–10, 11, 17, 28
hybridization, 50

International Society for Endangered Species (ISEC), 52
Iriomote cats, 33, *33*, 48
  habitat, 33
  prey, 33
  size, 33

jaguarundis, 41, *41*, 50

jungle cats, 8, 28–29, *28*
  prey, 28
  size, 28
  vocalizations, 29

kittens, 11, *11*
kodkods, 39–40

legs, 9
leopard cats, 31–32, *32*, 50
life span, 10
lynx, *9*, 24–25, *25*, 36, *42*, 47–48, *47*, 50

males, 10, 15, 18

marbled cats, 48

margays, 8, 37–38, *38*
  fur, 49
  habitat, 37–38, 48

mating season, 10, 11

money cats. *See* leopard cats.

mountain lions, 8

ocelots, *34*, 35–36, *37*, 50
  fur, 36, *49*

oncillas, 36–37
  fur, 49
  habitat, 36, 48

Pallas's cats, 27–28, *27*, 51
  fur, *27*, 49
  prey, 39
  Panthera genus, 8

predators, 10, 33, 37

retractable claws, 8

rusty-spotted cats, *6*, 7,
    26–27, *26*
  habitat, 26, 48

sand cats, 14–15, *14*, 50
  vocalizations, 15

servals, *12*, 17–18, *17*
  habitat, 17

prey, 17–18, *17*, 50
  size, 18

Siberian tigers, 7

small marbled cats, 32–
    33
  fur, 32
  habitat, 32
  prey, 32–33
  size, 32

Spanish lynx, 47–48, *47*
  habitat, 47
  prey, 47–48

speed, 9

teeth, 8, 9

Temminck's golden cats,
    30–31, *31*
  habitat, 30, 31, 48

territories, 10, 11, 15, 18,
    24–25

tiger cats. *See* oncillas.

tongues, 11

vocalizations, 15, 29

whiskers, 9

Wild About Cats, 51, 52

Wildlife Conservation
    Research Unit
    (WildCRU), 50

About the Author

Small Wildcats is Samantha Bonar's third book for Franklin Watts. Her previous titles are *Asteroids* and *Comets*. An editor at *The Los Angeles Times*, Ms. Bonar has also written for children's magazines, such as *American Girl, Boys' Life, Contact Kids, Highlights*, and *Owl*. Ms. Bonar lives in Southern California with her cat, Bear, and dog, Auggie.